CONTENTS

CREATING AN EMPIRE

During the 14th, 15th, and 16th centuries, the Aztec Empire ruled the part of **Mesoamerica** now known as central and southern Mexico. The early Aztecs, who called themselves the Mexica people, were once **nomadic**. According to legends, they wandered until they saw an eagle sitting on a cactus. It was eating a snake. The Aztec people saw this as a sign from one of their most important gods, Huitzilopochtli. They knew it was time to stop and build a city. This city—called Tenochtitlán—was founded in 1325. It became the center of the Aztec Empire. Today we know it as Mexico City, which is the capital of Mexico.

Daily life for a person living in the Aztec Empire depended on many factors, including their social class, profession, and gender. However, religion was a central part of daily life for all Aztec people.

Tenochtitlán was built on an island in Lake Texcoco. This map of the city was created after the Spanish conquered the Aztec people in the 16th century.

Heather Moore Niver

New York

Published in 2017 by The Rosen Publishing Group, Inc.
29 East 21st Street, New York, NY 10010

Editor: Katie Kawa
Book Design: Tanya Dellaccio

Photo Credits: Cover De Agostini/G. Dagli Orti/Getty Images; p. 5 UniversalImagesGroup/Getty Images; p. 6 https://commons.wikimedia.org/wiki/File:Codex_Mendoza_folio_20r.jpg; p. 7 https://commons.wikimedia.org/wiki/File:Houghton_Typ_625.99.800_Istoria_della_conquista_del_Messico_-_Motezuma.jpg; p. 8 https://commons.wikimedia.org/wiki/File:Feather_headdress_Moctezuma_II.JPG; pp. 9, 25 Dorling Kindersley/Getty Images; p. 11 DEA/A. DE GREGORIO/Getty Images; p. 12 (both) https://commons.wikimedia.org/wiki/File:Codex_Mendoza_folio_60r.jpg; p. 13 Felipe Davalos/Getty Images; p. 15 https://commons.wikimedia.org/wiki/File:Codex_Mendoza_folio_61r.jpg; pp. 16, 29 De Agostini Picture Library/Getty Images; p. 17 https://commons.wikimedia.org/wiki/File:Codex_Mendoza_folio_69r.jpg; p. 18 https://commons.wikimedia.org/wiki/File:Aztec_shared_meal.jpg; p. 19 (cocoa beans) Valentyn Volkov/Shutterstock.com; p. 19 (chili peppers and corn) Maks Narodenko/Shutterstock.com; p. 19 (tortilla) https://commons.wikimedia.org/wiki/File:NCI_flour_tortillas.jpg; p. 19 (avocado) Nataliia K/Shutterstock.com; p. 20 DONOT6_STUDIO/Shutterstock.com; p. 21 Werner Forman/Getty Images; p. 23 soft_light/Shutterstock.com; p. 27 fototehnik/Shutterstock.com.

Cataloging-in-Publication Data

Names: Niver, Heather Moore, author.
Title: Ancient Aztec daily life / Heather Moore Niver.
Description: New York : PowerKids Press, [2016] | Series: Spotlight on the Maya, Aztec, and Inca civilizations | Includes index.
Identifiers: LCCN 2016003621 | ISBN 9781499419009 (pbk.) | ISBN 9781499419030 (library bound) | ISBN 9781499419016 (6 pack)
Subjects: LCSH: Aztecs--Juvenile literature. | Aztecs--Social life and customs--Juvenile literature.
Classification: LCC F1219.73 .N57 2016 | DDC 972/.01--dc23
LC record available at http://lccn.loc.gov/2016003621

CPSIA Compliance Information: Batch ##BS16PK: For further information contact Rosen Publishing, New York, New York at 1-800-237-9932.

Santiago

POWERFUL PEOPLE

The Aztec Empire grew very powerful by conquering neighboring areas. Many groups of people were part of the Aztec Empire. The empire was made up of city-states, or independent states that consisted of a city and the areas surrounding it. An emperor ruled over the whole Aztec Empire. City-states that became part of the Aztec Empire paid the emperor a **tribute**. They offered him food, crafts, and men to serve as warriors.

This drawing of items used as tribute was found in an Aztec codex, or book of ancient writings.

The emperor was the most important member of Aztec society. Shown here is an illustration of the Aztec emperor Montezuma II.

The daily lives of Aztecs were directed by a system of social classes. The emperor was at the top, and there were three main classes of people below him. Nobles were military or political leaders and landowners. Priests could also be considered nobles. Commoners were farmers, merchants, craftspeople, and lesser priests. Slaves were the third major Aztec social class. An Aztec slave could buy his or her freedom.

CLOTHES AND CLASS

The Aztecs wore a wide variety of clothing. What they wore every day depended on their social class. Common people wore loose clothes that were most often made out of a fiber that came from the maguey plant. Women wove this into cloth. Girls learned to do this as they grew up.

Aztec nobles often wore clothing made from cotton. The Aztecs used natural dyes to make brightly colored clothes, which were generally worn only by nobles. The higher a person's social standing, the more decorations they wore on their clothing. The nobles wore decorations such as jewels and feathers. Jewelry was also an important part of what Aztecs wore, and the amount of jewelry a person wore

Aztec nobles—especially Aztec emperors—wore detailed headdresses with brightly colored feathers.

reflected their class. High-ranking members of Aztec society often wore jewelry made of gold and **turquoise**.

Common men and male slaves wore very little. It was better to wear less as they worked in the hot weather. Women of those classes wore long skirts.

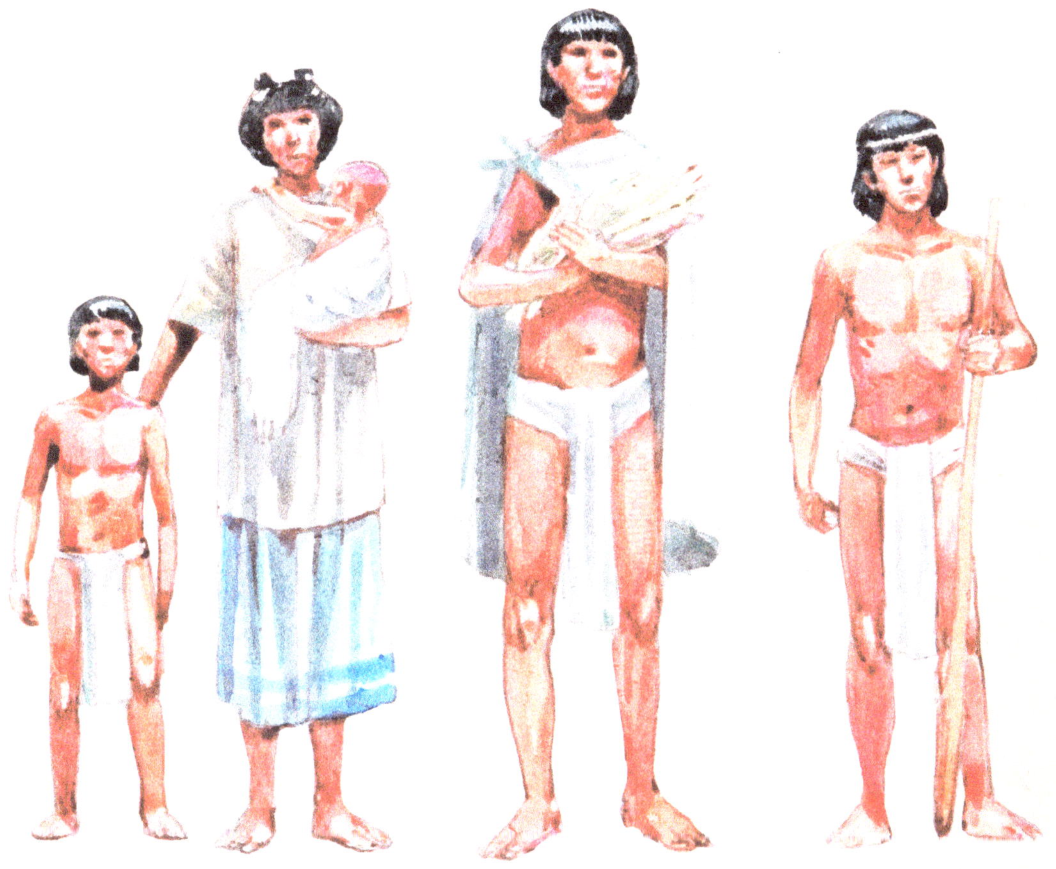

Members of the lower classes of Aztec society wore plain clothing. They weren't allowed to dress like nobles.

LIFE AS AN AZTEC KID

The Aztecs had a deep respect for war, and childbirth was seen as a kind of battle. In fact, if a woman died while giving birth, she was honored like a soldier who died fighting for the empire. It was believed she would go to a part of the afterlife reserved for those who died in battle. Births were celebrated with **rituals** in Aztec **culture**.

Aztec mothers and fathers were **strict**. Children were expected to do what their parents told them to do. Obedience was taught throughout the Aztec Empire, and children were punished in different ways for failing to do as they were told. Aztec children worked hard. Their parents taught them to do important tasks, including cooking meals and getting water.

Although Aztec children had to do chores every day, they had fun, too. When it was time to play, they enjoyed bow-and-arrow games, as well as playing with marbles and other simple toys.

This statue of a mother and child is believed to have been made by the Aztecs. While only male Aztecs could fight in wars, mothers in Aztec society were seen as their own kind of warrior.

SCHOOL DAYS

Aztec children also went to school. All Aztec children were educated. Children of commoners went to a school called a telpuchcalli. They learned basic skills for certain jobs, their rights and duties as Aztec citizens, history, and religion. Children from the lower classes who were very talented were sent to a school called a calmecac. Noble children went there, too. At this kind of school, Aztec children were trained to be priests or to work as government officials.

This page from an Aztec codex shows girls learning to weave and cook.

War was a common part of Aztec life. Boys born into the common class trained to be warriors, such as the ones shown here.

Boys and girls went to different schools. Boys were trained to be warriors if they went to a telpuchcalli. At a calmecac, they were taught to manage land and serve as leaders. Girls were commonly taught what they would need to know to be good wives, such as cooking, weaving, and playing a musical instrument. Some noble girls were sent to a school to learn from priestesses.

AZTEC WOMEN AND MARRIAGE

Aztec men were generally in control and held the power in society. Men were considered the heads of their households. An Aztec man could have multiple wives, but his first wife was generally his primary wife. This was more common among Aztec nobles than commoners. In a ruling family, only the children of the primary wife could **inherit** a leadership position.

Women in Aztec society weren't completely powerless, though. In fact, they sometimes had important jobs in the empire. Aztec women worked in marketplaces, and they served as priestesses. Some Aztec women also worked as **midwives**.

Aztec marriages were generally set up by family members. In some cases—especially among nobles—marriages were used for political gain and to create alliances. However, if a marriage failed for any number of reasons, Aztec men and women could ask a court for a legal separation.

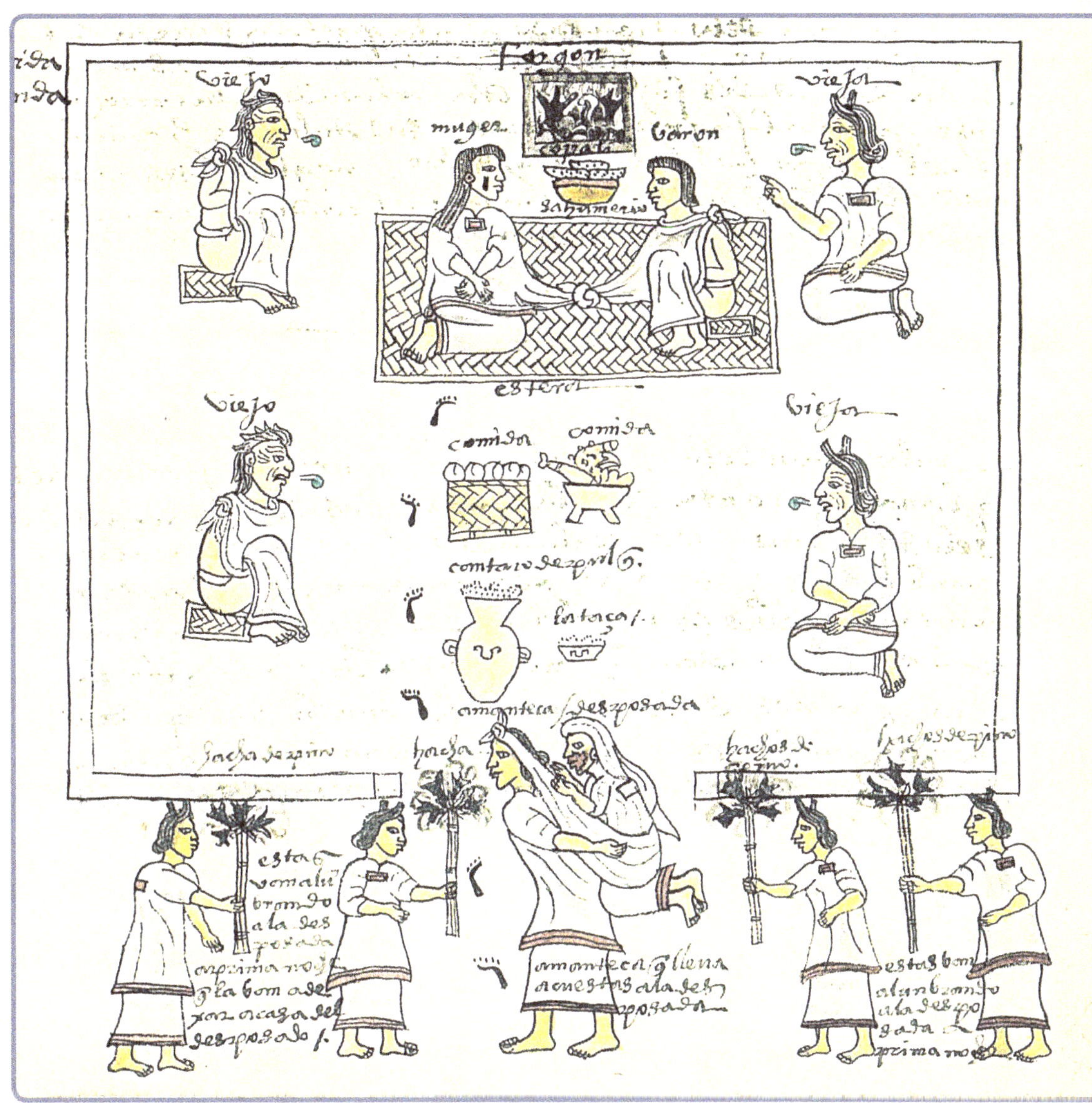

Shown here is part of an Aztec codex describing Aztec marriage rituals.

HOME SWEET HOME

Aztec people who were considered commoners lived in simple one-room or two-room homes. There was enough space for the people living in the house to sleep, cook, and eat. A **shrine** was made in the home so they could worship their gods. Because bathing was a very important part of Aztec life, Aztec homes often had a special room or a separate building on their land for getting clean. It was like a steam room.

AZTEC HOME

Shown here is a drawing of Emperor Montezuma II in his palace. Ruins of Aztec palaces and smaller houses have helped historians learn much about Aztec daily life and the places they called home.

Some Aztec homes were made of adobe. This is a kind of clay mixed with straw. It's formed into bricks that are left to dry and harden in the sun. The Aztec people were one of many groups living in what are now Central America, Mexico, and the southwestern United States to make homes out of adobe.

Aztec leaders lived in palaces. Aztec palaces had many more rooms than the homes commoners lived in.

TIME FOR DINNER!

Maize, or corn, was the most important food for the Aztec people. They ground it into a flour to bake into a kind of flat bread called a tortilla. Beans and squash were a frequent part of the Aztec diet, too. The Aztec people also ate many other fruits and vegetables, such as chili peppers, tomatoes, and avocados.

The Aztec people ate meat in addition to things they could grow. They hunted rabbits and deer for food. They also fished. Some Aztec people raised animals to eat, including dogs.

Shown here is a drawing from a codex of Aztec men sharing a meal.

The cacao bean was considered very valuable to the Aztec people. It's also sometimes called the cocoa bean, and it's used to make chocolate. The ancient Aztec people made a chocolate drink using these beans. Only nobles could have this drink. Common people most often drank water. Cacao beans were also used as a kind of currency, or money, among the Aztec people.

Many foods that were common parts of daily Aztec meals are still considered important ingredients in Mexican cooking today.

CREATIVE FARMING

The Aztec people couldn't have food without farming, so agriculture was an important part of Aztec daily life. The area where the Aztecs lived was challenging for farmers. Certain parts of the empire lacked the flat space needed to grow enough food to keep everyone fed. To fix this problem, Aztec farmers used a method called terrace farming. They made flat areas on hillsides to grow crops.

Terrace farming is a method of growing crops used all over the world!

The artificial islands known as chinampas can still be seen in parts of Mexico, such as Xochimilco, shown here.

Other areas were too wet and swampy to grow crops using traditional methods. Farmers dealt with this challenge by developing island gardens called chinampas. Chinampas allowed Aztec farmers to grow food in lakes, including Lake Texcoco. To make chinampas, they used materials found in the natural world around them. They took mud from the bottom of lakes and used this mud to create islands. Chinampas were known for their fertile soil, which allowed the Aztecs to grow many crops.

CRAFTS AND GAMES

Creativity was part of daily life for many Aztec people. Aztec **artisans** created goods, such as housewares and masks, from wood and clay. Others made baskets or wove cloth. Many Aztec artisans sold what they made in the marketplaces that existed in every city-state. Some Aztecs made jewelry—often for the nobility. Scribes wrote things down in the Aztec language.

Life wasn't all work for the Aztecs. They had a good time playing games, too. They had their own popular board game, which was called patolli. The Aztec people also played a game with a ball on a court. It was called *ullamaliztli* or tlachtli. Players could only move the ball around using their hips, shoulders, knees, and head. The object of the game was to get the ball through a stone hoop.

Many ancient Mesoamerican cultures played a sport similar to *ullamaliztli*. Shown here are the ruins of a ball court found where the ancient Maya city of Uxmal once stood.

RELIGION AND RITUALS

Religion was at the center of Aztec life. The Aztecs worshipped many gods. These gods were often connected to nature. Huitzilopochtli was the god of sun and war. Tonatiuh was also a god of the sun, and Tlaloc was the god of rain. Quetzalcóatl was the god of several things, including priesthood, learning, death, and rebirth. The Aztecs had many rituals and ceremonies for their gods.

Human sacrifice was practiced as part of the Aztec religion. The Aztecs believed they had to feed Huitzilopochtli human blood and hearts every day.

The Aztecs believed in an afterlife and **reincarnation**. They thought the way a person died helped decide what happened to them after death. For example, if a warrior died in battle or as a sacrifice, he was thought to go to a different part of the afterlife than someone who died of a disease.

The Aztecs built temples where they performed religious ceremonies. Temples were the most important buildings in Aztec city-states.

DAILY CALENDAR

The Aztec people kept track of their days with a calendar that was influenced by their religious beliefs. We know about the Aztec calendar because of a calendar stone discovered in Mexico City in 1790. It's called the Cuauhxicalli Eagle Bowl or the Sun Stone. It weighs around 25 tons (22.7 mt)! This calendar stone features a combination of art and math. Priests kept the calendar, which was dedicated to the sun god Tonatiuh. He's pictured at the center of the stone.

The Aztec calendar was actually two different calendars. One was for religious rituals, and it consisted of 260 days divided equally into 20 months. A different Aztec god ruled over each month. The other was a civil or solar calendar that consisted of 365 days. This calendar was divided into 18 months with 20 days in each month. The five days left over were believed to be unlucky days.

Some historians aren't sure the Sun Stone was actually a calendar in the way we think of calendars today. They believe it served as an altar for religious ceremonies, including human sacrifices.

AZTEC SUN STONE

THE END OF AN EMPIRE

Daily life as the Aztec people knew it changed drastically in 1519 when Hernán Cortés came to Aztec lands from Spain. He wasn't there for a friendly visit. He wanted to take over the land in the name of Spain. The Spanish had guns and horses that allowed them to conquer the Aztec people. They also spread diseases such as smallpox, which killed many Aztecs because they'd never been exposed to it before.

As the Spanish took over Aztec lands, they eventually captured Montezuma II, who was the Aztec emperor at that time. In 1521, the Spanish took over the city of Tenochtitlán.

Over time, new settlements and cities were built on the lands that were once Aztec city-states. Very few reminders of the Aztec Empire were left behind. However, the Spanish did keep written records of their experiences with the Aztec people. These writings have told us much about what daily life was like in the Aztec Empire.

Montezuma II was the Aztec emperor when Cortés and his men marched into Aztec lands. He died during the time of the Spanish conquest.

HERNÁN CORTÉS
MONTEZUMA II

A LOOK INTO AZTEC LIFE

Historians and archaeologists are working together to learn as much as possible about daily life in the Aztec Empire. They investigate the ruins of the homes where Aztec people once lived and other artifacts that have survived. Religious artifacts, pieces of pottery, and even gravesites have provided historians with important details about how different groups of Aztec people—from nobles to slaves—lived.

The daily lives of the Aztec people seem to have been ruled by very specific factors. Their religion ordered everything they did. Their society's structure also shaped everyday life. The daily life of a ruler was very different from a commoner's life. However, don't think that the Aztec people's focus on their gods and strict class system meant they were serious all the time. The Aztecs had time for celebrations, games, and fun, too!

GLOSSARY

artisan (AAR-tuh-zuhn): A skilled worker who makes things with their hands.

culture (KUHL-chuhr): The beliefs and ways of life of a certain group of people.

inherit (ihn-HEHR-uht): To get something, such as a title, after a person in your family dies.

Mesoamerica (meh-zoh-uh-MEHR-ih-kuh): The southern part of North America and part of Central America that was—at one time—occupied by people with shared cultural features, such as the Maya and Aztecs.

midwife (MIHD-wyf): A woman who helps other women during childbirth.

nomadic (noh-MAA-dihk): Having no fixed home and wandering from place to place.

reincarnation (ree-ihn-kaar-NAY-shuhn): The belief that, after death, people are reborn in new bodies or new forms of life.

ritual (RIH-chuh-wuhl): An established form of a ceremony.

shrine (SHRYN): A place built to honor someone or something.

strict (STRIHKT): Absolute, kept with great care.

tribute (TRIH-byoot): Payment by one ruler or nation to another as the price of peace.

turquoise (TUHR-koyz): A blue or bluish-green mineral used in jewelry.

INDEX

PRIMARY SOURCE LIST

Page 5: Map of Tenochtitlán. Contained in *General Atlas of All the Islands in the World by* Alonso de Santa Cruz. ca. 1560. Original now kept at the National Library of Spain, Madrid, Spain.

Page 6: Folio 20 of the Codex Mendoza. Creator unknown. ca. 1542. Now kept at the Bodleian Library, Oxford University, Oxford, UK.

Page 12 (both): Folio 60 of the Codex Mendoza. Creator unknown. ca. 1542. Now kept at the Bodleian Library, Oxford University, Oxford, UK.

Page 15: Folio 61 of the Codex Mendoza. Creator unknown. ca. 1542. Now kept at the Bodleian Library, Oxford University, Oxford, UK.

Page 17: Folio 69 of the Codex Mendoza. Creator unknown. ca. 1542. Now kept at the Bodleian Library, Oxford University, Oxford, UK.

WEBSITES

Due to the changing nature of Internet links, PowerKids Press has developed an online list of websites related to the subject of this book. This site is updated regularly. Please use this link to access the list: www.powerkidslinks.com/soac/azdl